Searchlight BOOKS™

What's Cool about Science?

Discover

Cryobiology

Lisa J. Amstutz

Lerner Publications ◆ Minneapolis

Content Consultant: Dayong Gao, Ph.D., Professor, University of Washington, Seattle

Lerner Publications Company
A division of Lerner Publishing Group, Inc.
241 First Avenue North
Minneapolis, MN 55401 USA

For reading levels and more information, look up this title at www.lernerbooks.com.

Library of Congress Cataloging-in-Publication Data

Names: Amstutz, Lisa J., author.
Title: Discover cryobiology / by Lisa J. Amstutz.
Description: Minneapolis : Lerner Publications, [2017] | Series: Searchlight books. What's cool about science? | Audience: Ages 8–11. | Audience: Grades 4–6. | Includes bibliographical references and index.
Identifiers: LCCN 2015047375 (print) | LCCN 2015049576 (ebook) | ISBN 9781512408072 (lb : alk. paper) | ISBN 9781512412840 (pb : alk. paper) | ISBN 9781512410631 (eb pdf)
Subjects: LCSH: Cryobiology—Juvenile literature. | Cryopreservation of organs, tissues, etc.—Juvenile literature. | Cold—Physiological effect—Juvenile literature.
Classification: LCC QH324.9.C7 A64 2017 (print) | LCC QH324.9.C7 (ebook) | DDC 571.4/645—dc23

LC record available at http://lccn.loc.gov/2015047375

Manufactured in the United States of America
1 – VP – 7/15/16

Contents

Chapter 1

WHAT IS CRYOBIOLOGY?

Cryobiology is the study of how cold affects living things. These things range from tiny cells to large animals. The first part of the word *cryobiology* comes from the Greek word *kryos*, which means "cold." The second part, *biology*, means "the study of life."

Cryobiologists wear protective gear. Where does the word *cryobiology* come from?

Cryobiology can help preserve tissues and organs so that doctors can save lives. It can help farmers breed better livestock. It can even help scientists save endangered animals.

Cold temperatures are useful for preserving many kinds of scientific samples.

Lessons from Nature

Cryobiologists study animals that live in cold places. These animals have special ways of surviving. The Arctic ground squirrel takes a seven-month nap! Its body temperature drops below the freezing point of water. But its cells do not freeze.

Arctic ground squirrels often begin their resting periods in late August.

This wood frog will remain frozen for up to eight months. Wood frogs live throughout Canada and the northeastern United States.

The wood frog, on the other hand, freezes solid in winter. Its heart and breathing stop as its body freezes. When the weather warms up, the frog's heart thaws first. The rest soon follows. It hops away healthy.

Robert Boyle studied how warm and cold temperatures affect gases.

The History of Cryobiology

Since ancient times, people have treated bleeding and swelling with ice. Early scientists, such as Robert Boyle, experimented with cold temperatures in the 1600s. But scientists had no way to make ice in the lab. The invention of refrigeration technology in the early 1800s changed this.

In the late 1800s, scientists learned to create liquid nitrogen. They did this by cooling the gas under high pressure. Now they could make things colder than ever before. Liquid nitrogen exists at a temperature of –321°F (–196°C). It is often used in cryobiology today.

LIQUID NITROGEN IS STORED IN SPECIALLY DESIGNED TANKS THAT KEEP IT COOL.

Uses of Cryobiology

When human cells freeze, sharp ice crystals tear them apart. This causes frostbite, which can lead to injury or even death. Many animal cells work the same way.

Skin that is exposed to cold temperatures can become frostbitten.

The adaptations of arctic animals teach scientists a lot about how to preserve living cells.

Scientists are finding ways to freeze cells safely. This would allow these cells to be preserved and stored for a long time. Scientists are learning from wood frogs and other animals that live in cold places.

FREEZING MATERIALS FROM LIVING THINGS IS ALREADY COMMON TODAY.

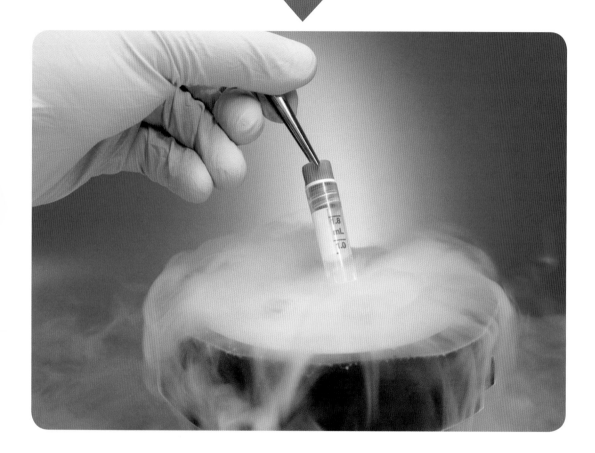

Today, scientists can freeze some cells, tissues, organs, and embryos. They can even use cold liquids to do surgery. Cryobiology has become one of the "coolest" fields of modern science!

Let It Snow!

Did you know that certain bacteria make it snow? These tiny organisms cause ice crystals to form. This creates snow at higher temperatures than usual. The bacteria are added to snowmaking machines at ski resorts. They are also sprayed into clouds to make it rain or snow.

Snowmaking machines have been in use since the 1950s.

Chapter 2

PRESERVING LIFE

Cold temperatures have important medical uses. Chilling blood and body parts preserves them. However, freezing can also damage these parts. New techniques are overcoming this problem.

Donated blood is stored in refrigerators. What other things can be preserved by keeping them cool?

At the same time, some scientists are working on even more advanced technology. They are looking for ways to freeze an entire person and revive him or her years in the future.

Frozen people could be safely stored in steel containers for years.

Large amounts of frozen blood are stored in places called blood banks.

Freezing Blood

Blood is one of the easiest tissues to freeze. Donated blood is usually refrigerated. But sometimes the blood is not needed right away. Freezing keeps it from being wasted.

Blood can be frozen for years. A chemical called a cryoprotectant agent, or CPA, is added. It prevents cells from swelling and bursting. The blood is thawed when it is ready for use. The CPA is taken out before the blood is given to a patient.

Blood samples frozen for research are often contained in small tubes.

Freezing Organs

Sometimes a person's heart, liver, or other organ stops working. Doctors replace the organ with one from another person. This is called an organ transplant.

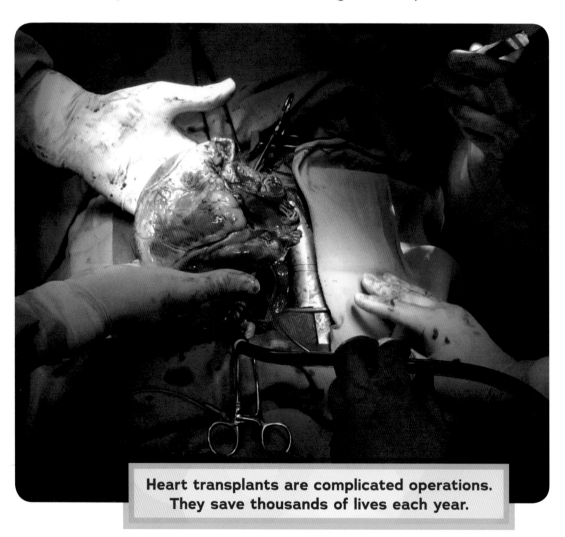

Heart transplants are complicated operations. They save thousands of lives each year.

Transplant organs are transferred in special coolers.

Each day, an average of seventy-nine people in the United States have organ transplants. But twenty-one more die because organs were not available. Most organs can't be stored very long unfrozen. A kidney can be kept for three days. A liver remains usable for thirty-six hours. Hearts or lungs last only six hours. If they could be frozen safely, they could be kept for years.

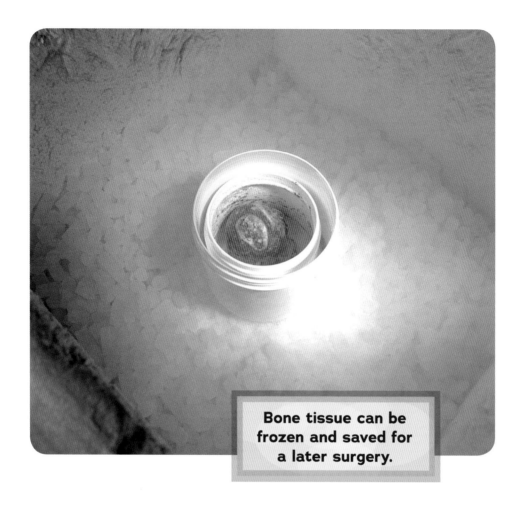

Bone tissue can be frozen and saved for a later surgery.

Scientists are unable to freeze most major organs. This includes the liver, heart, and lungs. However, some smaller organs and tissues can be frozen. These include heart valves, blood vessels, and parts of the knee. Skin can also be frozen. Freezing makes it much easier for patients to get the transplants they need.

Scientists use CPAs to freeze tissues. First, they add the CPA. Then they cool the tissue quickly. When the tissue is needed, they warm it and remove the CPA. It is important to freeze and thaw the cells at just the right speed. This stops ice from forming and damaging them.

Adding a CPA is critical to the preservation process.

The Arctic wooly bear caterpillar is one animal that creates its own CPA.

New Ways to Freeze

To learn how to freeze more kinds of organs safely, scientists study life in the coldest places on Earth. Many insects, reptiles, and polar fish survive winter by supercooling. A few mammals, such as the Arctic ground squirrel, do the same. These animals can lower their body temperatures without the water inside them turning to ice.

Supercooling is possible because water doesn't always freeze at 32°F (0°C). If it is very pure, it can be cooled to about −40°F (−40°C) before ice forms. This technique could keep organs healthy without creating harmful ice crystals.

Jagged ice crystals can damage organs and tissues.

Another cutting-edge freezing technique is called vitrification. This process cools cells so fast that ice crystals do not have time to form. The liquid inside gets thick, almost like a solid. It is similar to glass. It has no sharp ice crystals to tear cell walls. Scientists can now vitrify blood vessels and other small tissues. Some have already vitrified and transplanted rabbit kidneys.

VITRIFICATION IS CARRIED OUT IN SPECIALIZED LABORATORIES.

Antifreeze in Fish Blood

Temperatures in the Arctic Ocean often drop below the normal freezing point of water. The salt in the water makes this possible. Polar fish survive by making antifreeze chemicals in their blood. These chemicals stop ice crystals from forming. Scientists have used antifreeze proteins from Arctic fish to freeze rat hearts safely.

Fish living in cold waters have adaptations to help them survive.

Someday organs may be stored as easily as blood is today.

Someday, we may be able to keep banks of frozen organs. New freezing technology will keep donated organs from going to waste. It will make it easier to match patients with the organs they need.

Life after Death?

For hundreds of years, people have tried to overcome death. Some think they have found the solution in cryonics. Cryonics is the process of freezing human bodies or heads. Supporters hope that someday the frozen people can be brought back to life.

The cryonics company Alcor stores its patients in tall metal tubes.

After the person dies of an injury or disease, his or her blood is drained and replaced with CPA. To bring these people back to life, scientists would replace the blood. Then they would need to fix any damaged cells. They would also need to fix whatever disease or injury killed the person.

Cryonics companies use liquid nitrogen, stored in huge tanks, to keep the bodies of their patients cool.

At the Cryonics Institute in Michigan, the families of preserved people sometimes leave flowers outside their loved ones' containers.

This technology is still extremely young. Most scientists do not believe it is possible right now. But that doesn't stop people from trying. There are already several hundred frozen bodies and brains in storage. If future scientists discover how to thaw and cure them, those people may live again.

Chapter 3

FREEZING NEW LIFE

Cold temperatures can also be used to store embryos. An embryo is a developing animal. It has not yet been born. At the Jackson Laboratory in Maine, scientists freeze mouse embryos. The embryos carry genes for diseases, such as cancer. When they are needed for research, the embryos can be thawed and grown inside a female mouse. Growing mice only when they are needed saves research money.

Storing animal embryos is useful for research. What is an embryo?

Frozen embryos can also be used to breed farm animals. For example, the eggs of a prize dairy cow can be collected. They are grown into embryos in the lab and frozen until they are needed. Then they are put into other cows. In this way, one cow can have many calves in the same year.

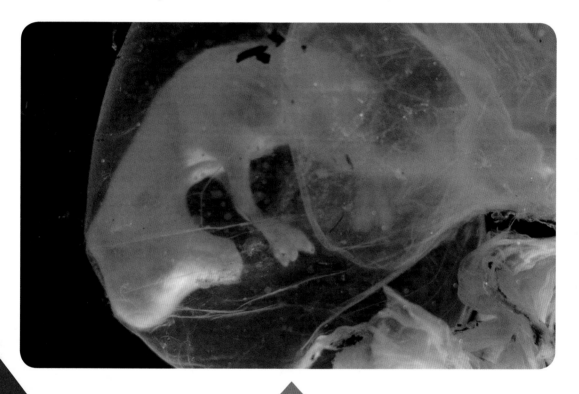

COW EMBRYOS DEVELOP FOR ABOUT NINE AND A HALF MONTHS BEFORE BEING BORN.

Freezing embryos and other cells can even help save endangered species. When there are only a few animals of a species left, a disease or other disaster could make them extinct. Using frozen cells, scientists can grow and release more animals into the wild. This method has already helped save the black-footed ferret. It is helping save giant pandas, Brazilian ocelots, and other species as well.

THE BLACK-FOOTED FERRET LIVES IN CENTRAL NORTH AMERICA.

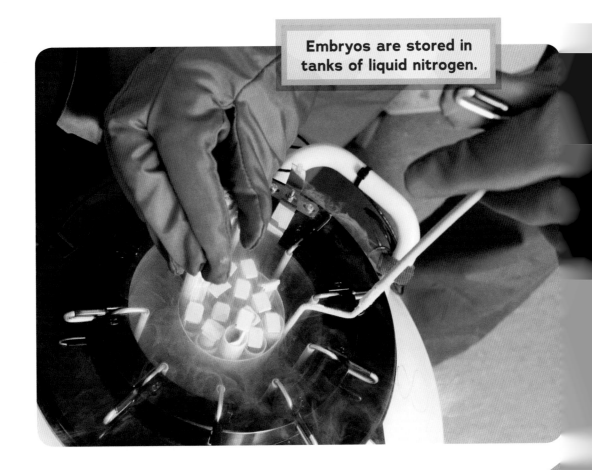

Embryos are stored in tanks of liquid nitrogen.

Growing Humans

Human embryos can be frozen too. They can be grown in labs. Some of the water is removed from the cells and replaced with CPAs. Then the embryos are stored until needed. The thawed embryos can grow into a baby inside a woman's body. This can help people who could not have children otherwise.

Chapter 4

COLD TREATMENTS

Sometimes doctors want to kill diseased cells. They use liquid nitrogen to treat warts and skin problems. They can also use it to treat cancer on the skin or inside the body. The cold liquid is dabbed or sprayed onto an area. It kills the cells, which then drop off. Freezing is fast, easy, and causes less scarring than cutting does. This type of surgery is called cryosurgery.

Extreme cold has been used to treat cancer in the kidneys.

Cold Surgery

During heart surgery, doctors often cool the patient's body. That way, the heart and brain need less oxygen. They can survive longer without damage.

Doctors are studying a new treatment for patients who suffer a heart attack after a severe injury. They remove the patient's blood and replace it with a cold, salty solution. The body temperature drops as low as 50°F (10°C). After surgery, the blood is replaced and the body is warmed up again.

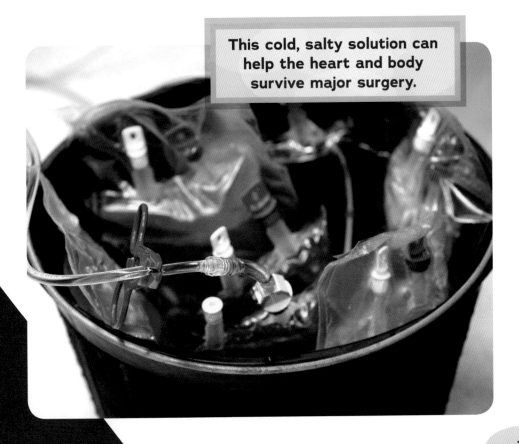

This cold, salty solution can help the heart and body survive major surgery.

Today's cryobiologists are changing our understanding of how cold temperatures can affect living things.

A Frozen Future?

Cryobiology is an exciting field of study. Perhaps someday we will have freezers full of organs, ready to be transplanted. Frozen embryos may bring back endangered species.

Other ideas seem far-fetched. Will cryonics patients ever be brought back to life? Could astronauts be frozen for long trips to far-off planets? No one knows for sure. But the future of cryobiology is likely to hold many exciting breakthroughs.

Frozen Zoos

Can you imagine an entire zoo that fits in one room? The San Diego Frozen Zoo stores frozen cells and tissues from nearly one thousand species of rare animals. Perhaps someday these animals will again roam the rain forests or plains.

Stored tissues may one day allow scientists to bring extinct animals back to life.

Glossary

antifreeze: a substance used to lower the freezing point of water

bacteria: microscopic, one-celled organisms

cryonics: the freezing of human bodies to preserve and possibly revive them in the future

cryoprotectant agent (CPA): a substance used to protect cells from damage during freezing and thawing

endangered: threatened with extinction

hibernate: to spend the winter in a dormant condition

organ: a group of tissues in an animal's body that serves a specific function, such as a heart or liver

supercool: to cool a liquid below its freezing point without forming crystals

tissue: a group of cells in an animal's body that performs a specific function

vitrify: to turn a liquid into a smooth, glass-like form

LERNER

Expand learning beyond the printed book. Download free, complementary educational resources for this book from our website, www.lerneresource.com.

SOURCE

Learn More about Cryobiology

Books

Marquardt, Meg. *Discover Cutting-Edge Medicine*. Minneapolis, MN: Lerner Publications, 2017. Learn more about the cutting-edge science behind modern organ transplants.

Rodríguez, Ana Maria. *Polar Bears, Penguins, and Other Mysterious Animals of the Extreme Cold*. Berkeley Heights, NJ: Enslow Publishers, Inc., 2012. Find out how polar bears, penguins, and other animals have adapted to extreme environments in the Arctic and Antarctic.

Winner, Cherie. *Circulating Life: Blood Transfusion from Ancient Superstition to Modern Medicine*. Minneapolis, MN: Twenty-First Century Books, 2007. Learn more about the history and science of blood transfusions.

Websites

How Stuff Works: Cryonics
http://science.howstuffworks.com/life/genetic/cryonics.htm
Discover the history and science of cryonics research.

National Geographic: How Wood Frogs Survive Being Frozen Alive
http://voices.nationalgeographic.com/2013/08/21/how-the-alaska-wood-frog-survives-being-frozen
Find out how wood frogs freeze in winter and thaw out again unharmed.

National Park Service: Arctic Ground Squirrel
http://www.nps.gov/dena/learn/nature/arcticgroundsquirrel.htm
Learn more about how Arctic ground squirrels hibernate during the frigid Arctic winter.

Index

Photo Acknowledgments

The images in this book are used with the permission of: © choja/iStock.com, pp. 4, 36; © fotografixx/iStock.com, p. 5; © Susan Sterna/iStock.com, p. 6; © Ted Kinsman/Science Source, p. 7; © Science Source, p. 8; © Michael Krinke/iStock.com, p. 9; © ArtShotPhoto/Shutterstock.com, p. 10; © outdoorsman/Shutterstock.com, p. 11; © dra_schwartz/iStock.com, p. 12; © Cameron Strathdee/iStock.com, p. 13; © 21597185/iStock.com, p. 14; © Michael Macor/San Francisco Chronicle/Corbis, p. 15; © Laurent/Science Source, p. 16; © Jammy Photography/Shutterstock.com, p. 17; © Jamie-Andrea Yanak/AP Images, p. 18; © Hemera Technologies/PhotoObjects.net/Thinkstock, p. 19; © Colin Cuthbert/Science Source, p. 20; © BSIP/Newscom, pp. 21, 35; © Louise Murray/Science Source, p. 22; © Dan Bach Kristensen/Shutterstock.com, p. 25; © Eric Strand/Shutterstock.com, p. 23; © Elena Pavlovich/Shutterstock.com, p. 24; © Serpil_Borlu/iStock.com, p. 26; © Irwin Daugherty/East Valley Tribune/AP Images, p. 27; © Isaac74/Shutterstock.com, p. 28; © MORVAN/SIPA/Newscom, p. 29; © Monkey Business Images/Shutterstock.com, p. 30; © Daniel Sambraus/Science Source, p. 31; Ryan Moehring/USFWS, p. 32; © Medicimage/Science Source, p. 33; © Laurent Belmonte/Science Source, p. 34; © Shankar Vedentam/KRT/Newscom, p. 37.

Front Cover: © Pasquale Sorrentino/Science Source.

Main body text set in Adrianna Regular 14/20.
Typeface provided by Chank.